Arranged and Introduced
by the Rector of
the National Shrine of The Divine Mercy

MARIAN PRESS
STOCKBRIDGE MA 01263

The National Shrine of The Divine Mercy
An Imprint of Marian Press
2004

Available from:

National Shrine of
The Divine Mercy
2 Prospect Hill
Stockbridge, MA 01262
413-298-3931
e-mail: shrine@marian.org

Shrine Gift Shop
P.O. Box 559
Stockbridge, MA 01262
1-888-484-1112
e-mail: giftshop@marian.org

Marian Helpers Center
Eden Hill
Stockbridge, MA 01263
Prayerline: 1-800-804-3823
Orderline: 1-800-462-7426
Website: www.marian.org

Typesetting: Patricia Menatti
Cover Design: Bill Sosa

Front Cover: Artwork of Jesus carrying His cross © Congregation of Marians of the Immaculate Conception. Courtesy of Marian Archives.

Inside Front and Inside Back covers: Photos of stained glass window and crucifix in the National Shrine of The Divine Mercy © Congregation of Marians of the Immaculate Conception. Courtesy of Marian Archives.

For text from the English Edition of
Diary of St. Maria Faustina Kowalska:

NIHIL OBSTAT:
George H. Pearce, SM
Former Archbishop of Suva, Fiji

IMPRIMATUR:
Joseph F. Maguire
Bishop of Springfield, MA
April 9, 1984

The NIHIL OBSTAT and IMPRIMATUR are a declaration that a book, booklet, or pamphlet is considered to be free from doctrinal or moral error. It is not implied that those who have granted the NIHIL OBSTAT or IMPRIMATUR agree with the contents, opinions, or statements expressed.

ISBN: 0-944203-73-6

Printed with permission of the Congregation of Sisters of Our Lady of Mercy.

Printed in the United States of America by Marian Press

TABLE OF CONTENTS

INTRODUCTION

It is with great joy that I introduce to you *St. Faustina's Way of the Cross* Prayerbook. For several years, my staff used a similar booklet to pray this unique Stations of the Cross daily with the pilgrims who visited the National Shrine of The Divine Mercy. Due to the overwhelming number of requests for this prayerbook, I sought copyright permission from St. Faustina's community of religious sisters, the Congregation of Sisters of Our Lady of Mercy in Cracow, Poland. They have graciously authorized us to print and distribute this book.

I truly believe you will find *St. Faustina's Way of the Cross* exceptional, because it will lead you to reflect on the Lord's Passion through the eyes and heart of St. Faustina — our Lord's secretary of mercy. With each station, along with a verse of Sacred Scripture, the priest speaks the words of Jesus and the people those of St. Faustina. (These words are taken directly from the *Diary of St. Faustina*). It is amazing to contemplate how this Mercy Saint, who suffered so much, was called to share in the Lord's Passion. By praying *St. Faustina's Way of the Cross* we, too, are inspired to enter into this beautiful mystery.

Saint Faustina herself found tremendous solace in meditating on the Lord's Passion — especially at the three o'clock hour. In her *Diary*, Jesus repeatedly asked St. Faustina to immerse herself in His Passion. "My daughter, try to make the Stations of the Cross in this hour, provided that your duties permit it" (*Diary*, 1572).

My personal prayer is that this booklet will assist you in contemplating our Lord's Passion and His unfathomable mercy. I pray that by St. Faustina's intercession you may surrender yourself more deeply to our merciful Lord, who accepted the cross for you.

By the Rector of the National Shrine of The Divine Mercy

The Way of The Cross

Opening Prayer

All: Merciful Lord, my Master, I want to follow You faithfully. I want to imitate You in my life in an ever more perfect way. That is why I ask that by meditating on Your Passion, You would grant me the grace of a deeper understanding of the mysteries of the spiritual life.

Mary, Mother of Mercy, always faithful to Christ, lead me in the footsteps of the sorrowful Passion of your Son and ask for me the necessary graces for a fruitful making of this Way of the Cross.

Sung Verse*:   *At the cross her station keeping*
Stood the mournful Mother weeping
Close to Jesus to the last.

* Verses taken from the hymn STABAT MATER.

First Station: Jesus Is Condemned to Die

Celebrant: We adore You, O Christ, and we praise You.

People: Because by Your holy Cross and Resurrection, You have redeemed the world.

Celebrant: The chief priests and the entire Sanhedrin kept trying to obtain false testimony against Jesus in order to put Him to death, but they found none, though many false witnesses came forward (Matthew 26:59-60).

Jesus: (Celebrant) **Do not be surprised that you are sometimes unjustly accused. I Myself first drank this cup of undeserved suffering for love of you** (289). **When I was before Herod, I obtained a grace for you; namely, that you would be able to rise above human scorn and follow faithfully in My footsteps** (1164).

S. Faustina: (People) We are sensitive to words and quickly want to answer back, without taking any regard as to whether it is

God's will that we should speak. A silent soul is strong; no adversities will harm it if it perseveres in silence. The silent soul is capable of attaining the closest union with God (477).

All: Merciful Jesus, help me to know how to accept every human judgment and do not allow me ever to render a condemnatory judgment on You in my neighbors.

C. You, who suffered wounds for us,

P. Christ Jesus, have mercy on us.

Sung Verse: *Through her heart, His sorrow sharing*
All His bitter anguish bearing
Now at length the sword has passed.

Second Station:
Jesus Carries His Cross

C. We adore You, O Christ, and we praise You.

P. Because by Your holy Cross and Resurrection, You have redeemed the world.

C. Then Pilate took Jesus and had Him scourged. And the soldiers wove a crown out of thorns and placed it on His head, and clothed Him in a purple cloak, and they came to Him and said, "Hail, King of the Jews!" So Jesus came out, wearing the crown of thorns and the purple cloak. And Pilate said to them, "Behold, the man!" When the chief priests and the guards saw Him they cried out, "Crucify Him, crucify Him!" (John 19:1-6).

Jesus: (C.) **Do not be afraid of sufferings; I am with you** (151). **The more you will come to love suffering, the purer your love for Me will be** (279).

S. Faustina: (P.) Jesus, I thank You for the little daily crosses, for opposition to my endeavors, for the hardships of communal life, for the misinterpretation of my intentions, for humiliations at the hands of others, for the harsh way in which we are treated, for false suspicions, for poor health and loss of strength, for self-denial, for dying to myself, for lack of recognition in everything, for the upsetting of all my plans. (343).

All: Merciful Jesus, teach me to value life's toil, sicknesses, and every suffering, and with love to carry my daily crosses.

C. You, who suffered wounds for us,
P. Christ Jesus, have mercy on us.

Sung Verse: *O, how sad and sore distressed*
Was that Mother highly blessed
of the sole Begotten One.

Third Station:
Jesus Falls the First Time

C. We adore You, O Christ, and we praise You.

P. Because by Your holy Cross and Resurrection, You have redeemed the world.

C. We had all gone astray like sheep, each following his own way; But the Lord laid upon Him the guilt of us all (Isaiah 53:6, 12).

Jesus: (C.) **Involuntary offenses of souls do not hinder My love for them or prevent Me from uniting Myself with them. But voluntary offenses, even the smallest, obstruct My graces, and I cannot lavish My gifts on such souls** (1641).

S. Faustina: (P.) My Jesus, despite Your graces, I see and feel all my misery … O my Jesus, how prone I am to evil, and this forces me to be constantly vigilant. But I do not lose heart. I trust God's grace, which abounds in the worst misery (606).

All: Merciful Lord, preserve me from every, even the tiniest but voluntary and conscious infidelity.

C. You, who suffered wounds for us,

P. Christ Jesus, have mercy on us.

Sung Verse: *Is there one who would not weep, Whelmed in miseries so deep Christ's dear Mother to behold?*

Fourth Station:
Jesus Meets His Sorrowful Mother

C. We adore You, O Christ, and we praise You.

P. Because by Your holy Cross and Resurrection, You have redeemed the world.

C. Behold, this child is destined for the fall and rise of many in Israel, and to be a sign that will be contradicted so that the thoughts of many hearts may be revealed. And you yourself a sword will pierce (Luke 2:34-35).

Jesus: (C.) **Although all the works that come into being by My will are exposed to great sufferings, consider whether any of them has been subject to greater difficulties than that work which is directly Mine — the work of Redemption. You should not worry too much about adversities.** (1643).

S. Faustina: (P.) I saw the Blessed Virgin, unspeakable beautiful. She held me close to herself and said to me, I *am Mother to you all, thanks to the unfathomable mercy of God. Most pleasing to me is that soul which faithfully carries out the will of God. Be courageous. Do not fear apparent obstacles, but fix your gaze upon the Passion of my Son, and in this way you will be victorious* (449).

All: Mary, Mother of Mercy, be near me always, especially in suffering as you were on your Son's way of the cross.

C. You, who suffered wounds for us,

P. Christ Jesus, have mercy on us.

Sung Verse: *Can the human heart refrain*
                     From partaking in her pain
                     In that Mother's pain untold?

Fifth Station:
Simon Helps Jesus Carry His Cross

C. We adore You, O Christ, and we praise You.

P. Because by Your holy Cross and Resurrection, You have redeemed the world.

C. As they led Him away they took hold of a certain Simon, a Cyrenian, who was coming in from the country; and after laying the cross on him, they made him carry it behind Jesus (Luke 23:26).

Jesus: (C.) **Write that by day and by night My gaze is fixed upon him, and I permit these adversities in order to increase your merit. I do not reward for good results but for the patience and hardship undergone for My sake** (86).

S. Faustina: (P.) Jesus, You do not give a reward for the successful performance of a work, but for the good will and the labor undertaken. Therefore, I am completely at peace, even if all my undertakings and efforts should be thwarted or should come to naught. If I do all that is in my power, the rest is not my business (952).

All: Jesus, my Lord, let my every thought, word, and deed be undertaken exclusively out of love for You. Keep on cleansing my intentions.

C. You, who suffered wounds for us,

P. Christ Jesus, have mercy on us.

Sung Verse: *Let me share with thee His pain*
Who for all my sins was slain,
Who for me in torments died.

Sixth Station:
Veronica Wipes the Face of Jesus

C. We adore You, O Christ, and we praise You.

P. Because by Your holy Cross and Resurrection, You have redeemed the world.

C. He grew up like a sapling before him, like a shoot from the parched earth; There was in Him no stately bearing to make us look at Him, no appearance that would attract us to Him. He was spurned and avoided by men, a man of suffering, accustomed to infirmity. One of those from whom men hide their faces spurned, and we held Him in no esteem (Isaiah 53:2-3).

Jesus: (C.) **Know that whatever good you do to any soul, I accept it as if you had done it to Me** (1768).

S. Faustina: (P.) I am learning how to be good from Jesus, from Him who is goodness itself, so that I may be called a [child] of the heavenly Father (669). Great love can change small things into great ones, and it is only love which lends value to our actions (303).

All: Lord Jesus, my Master, grant that my eyes, my hands, my lips and my heart may always be merciful. Transform me into mercy.

C. You, who suffered wounds for us,

P. Christ Jesus, have mercy on us.

Sung Verse: *Let me mingle tears with thee,*
                Mourning   Him   who
                mourned for me,
                All the days that I may live.

Seventh Station: Jesus Falls the Second Time

C. We adore You, O Christ, and we praise You.

P. Because by Your holy Cross and Resurrection, You have redeemed the world.

C. Yet it was our infirmities that He bore, our sufferings that He endured, while we thought of Him as stricken, as one smitten by God and afflicted (Isaiah 53:4).

Jesus: (C.) **The cause of your falls is that you rely too much upon yourself and too little on Me. But let this not sadden you so much. You are dealing with the God of mercy** (1488). **Know that of yourself you can do nothing** (639). **Without special help from Me, you are not even capable of accepting My graces** (738).

S. Faustina: (P.) Jesus, do not leave me alone in suffering. You know, Lord, how weak I am. I am an abyss of wretchedness, I am nothingness itself; so what will be so strange if You leave me alone and I fall?

(1489). So You, Jesus, must stand by me constantly like a mother by a helpless child — and even more so (264).

All: May Your grace assist me, Lord, that I may not keep falling continuously into the same faults; and when I fall, help me to rise and glorify Your mercy.

C. You, who suffered wounds for us,

P. Christ Jesus, have mercy on us.

Sung Verse: *Make me feel as thou hast felt;*
Make my soul to glow and melt
With the love of Christ my Lord.

Eighth Station:
Jesus Meets the
Women of Jerusalem

C. We adore You, O Christ, and we praise You.

P. Because by Your holy Cross and Resurrection, You have redeemed the world.

C. A large crowd of people followed Jesus, including many women who mourned and lamented Him. Jesus turned to them and said, "Daughters of Jerusalem, do not weep for Me; weep instead for yourselves and for your children (Luke 23: 27-28).

Jesus: (C.) **O how pleasing to Me is living faith!** (1420) **Tell all, that I demand that they live in the spirit of faith** (353).

S. Faustina: (P.) I fervently beg the Lord to strengthen my faith, so that in my drab, everyday life I will not be guided by human dispositions, but by those of the spirit. Oh, how everything drags man towards the earth! But lively faith maintains the soul in the higher regions and assigns self-love its proper place; that is to say, the lowest one (210).

All: Merciful Lord, I thank You for holy Baptism and the grace of faith. Continuously, I call: Lord, I believe, increase my faith.

C. You, who suffered wounds for us,

P. Christ Jesus, have mercy on us.

Sung Verse: *O thou Mother! Fount of love!*
Touch my spirit from above,
Make my heart with thine accord.

Ninth Station:
Jesus Falls the Third Time

C. We adore You, O Christ, and we praise You.

P. Because by Your holy Cross and Resurrection, You have redeemed the world.

C. Though He was harshly treated, He submitted and opened not His mouth. Like a lamb led to the slaughter or a sheep before the shearers, He was silent and opened not His mouth. Oppressed and condemned, He was taken away, and who would have thought any more of His destiny? When He was cut off from the land of the living, and smitten for the sin of His people, a grave was assigned Him among the wicked and a burial place with evildoers, though He had done no wrong nor spoken any falsehood. But the Lord was pleased to crush Him in infirmity. If He gives His life as an offering for sin He shall see His decendants in a long life, and the will of the Lord shall be accomplished through Him. Because of His affliction He shall see the light in fullness of days (Isaiah 53:7-10).

Jesus: (C.) **My child, know that the greatest obstacles to holiness are discour-**

22

agement and an exaggerated anxiety. These will deprive you of the ability to practice virtue. Do not lose heart in coming for pardon, for I am always ready to forgive you. As often as you beg for it, you glorify My mercy. (1488).

S. Faustina: (P.) My Jesus, despite Your graces, I see and feel all my misery. I begin my day with battle and end it with battle. As soon as I conquer one obstacle, ten more appear to take its place. But I am not worried, because I know that this is the time of struggle, not peace (606).

All: Merciful Lord, I give over to You that which is my exclusive property, that is, my sin and my human weakness. I beg You, may my misery drown in Your unfathomable mercy.

C. You, who suffered wounds for us,

P. Christ Jesus, have mercy on us.

Sung Verse: *Wounded with His ev'ry wound*
                 Steep my soul till it hath swooned
                 In His very Blood away.

Tenth Station:
Jesus Is Stripped of His Garments

C. We adore You, O Christ, and we praise You.

P. Because by Your holy Cross and Resurrection, You have redeemed the world.

C. When the soldiers had crucified Jesus, they took His clothes and divided them into four shares, a share for each soldier. They also took His tunic, but the tunic was seamless, woven in one piece from the top down. So they said to one another, "Let's not tear it, but cast lots for it to see whose it will be," in order that the passage of scripture might be fulfilled (John 19:23-24).

S. Faustina: (P.) Jesus was suddenly standing before me, stripped of His clothes, His body completely covered with wounds, His eyes flooded with tears and blood, His face disfigured and covered with spittle.

Jesus: (C.) **The bride must resemble her Betrothed.**

S. Faustina: (P.) I understood these words to their very depth. There is no room for doubt here. My likeness to Jesus must be through suffering and humility (268).

All: Jesus, meek and humble of heart, make my heart like unto Your heart.

C. You, who suffered wounds for us,

P. Christ Jesus, have mercy on us.

Sung Verse: *Bruised, derided, cursed, defiled,*
She beheld her tender Child
All with bloody scourges rent

Eleventh Station:
Jesus Is Nailed to the Cross

C. We adore You, O Christ, and we praise You.

P. Because by Your holy Cross and Resurrection, You have redeemed the world.

C. Those passing by reviled Him, shaking their heads and saying, "You would destroy the temple and rebuild it in three days, save Yourself, if You are the Son of God, [and] come down from the cross!" Likewise the chief priests with the scribes and elders mocked Him and said, "He saved others; He cannot save Himself. He trusted in God; let Him deliver Him now if he wants Him. For He said, 'I am the Son of God' " (Matthew 27:39-43).

Jesus: (C.) **My pupil, have great love for those who cause you suffering. Do good to those who hate you** (1628).

S. Faustina: (P.) O my Jesus, you know what efforts are needed to live sincerely and unaffectedly with those from whom our nature flees, or with those who, deliberately or not, have made us suffer. Humanly speaking, this is impossible. At such times more than at others, I try to discover the Lord Jesus in such a person and for the same Jesus, I do everything for such people (766).

All: O purest Love, rule in all Your plenitude in my heart and help me to do Your holy will most faithfully (328).

C. You, who suffered wounds for us,

P. Christ Jesus, have mercy on us.

Sung Verse: *Holy Mother! pierce me through;*
In my heart each wound renew
Of my Savior crucified.

Twelfth Station:
Jesus Dies on the Cross

C. We adore You, O Christ, and we praise You.

P. Because by Your holy Cross and Resurrection, You have redeemed the world.

C. But when they came to Jesus and saw that He was already dead, they did not break His legs, but one soldier thrust his lance into His side, and immediately blood and water flowed out (John 19:33-40).

Jesus: (C.) **All this is for the salvation of souls. Consider well, My daughter, what you are doing for their salvation (1184).**

S. Faustina: (P.) Then I saw the Lord Jesus nailed to the cross. When He had hung on it for a while, I saw a multitude of souls crucified like Him. Then I saw a second multitude of souls, and a third. The second multitude were not nailed to [their] crosses, but were holding them firmly in their hands. The third were neither nailed to [their] crosses nor holding them firmly in their hands, but were dragging [their] crosses behind them and were discontent.

Jesus: (C.) **Do you see these souls? Those who are like Me in the pain and contempt they suffer will be like Me also in glory. And those who resemble Me less in pain and contempt will also bear less resemblance to Me in glory (446).**

All: Jesus, my Savior, hide me in the depth of Your heart that, fortified by Your grace, I may be able to resemble You in the love of the Cross and have a share in Your glory.

C. You, who suffered wounds for us,
P. Christ Jesus, have mercy on us.

Sung Verse: *For the sins of His own nation,*
Saw Him hang in desolation
Till His Spirit forth He sent.

Thirteenth Station:
Jesus Is Taken Down
from the Cross

C. We adore You, O Christ, and we praise You.

P. Because by Your holy Cross and Resurrection, You have redeemed the world.

C. The centurion who witnessed what had happened glorified God and said, "This man was innocent beyond doubt." When all the people who had gathered for this spectacle saw what had happened, they returned home beating their breasts; but all His acquaintances stood at a distance, including the women who had followed Him from Galilee, and saw these events (Luke 23:47-49).

Jesus: (C.) **Most dear to Me is the soul that strongly believes in My goodness and has complete trust in Me. I heap My confidence upon it and give it all it asks** (453).

S. Faustina: (P.) I fly to Your mercy, Compassionate God, who alone are good. Although my misery is great, and my offenses are many, I trust in Your mercy, because You are the God of mercy; and, from time immemorial, it has never been heard of, nor do heaven or earth remember, that a soul trusting in Your mercy has been disappointed (1730).

All: Merciful Jesus, daily increase my trust in Your mercy that always and everywhere I may give witness to Your boundless goodness and love.

C. You, who suffered wounds for us,

P. Christ Jesus, have mercy on us.

Sung Verse: *Virgin of all virgins blest!*
Listen to my fond request:
Let me share your grief divine.

Fourteenth Station:
Jesus Is Placed in the Sepulchre

C. We adore You, O Christ, and we praise You.

P. Because by Your holy Cross and Resurrection, You have redeemed the world.

C. They took the body of Jesus and bound It with burial cloths along with the spices, according to the Jewish burial custom. Now in the place where He had been crucified there was a garden, and in the garden a new tomb, in which no one had yet been buried. So they laid Jesus there because of the Jewish preparation day; for the tomb was close by (John 19:38-42).

Jesus: (C.) **But child, you are not yet in your homeland; so go, fortified by My grace, and fight for My kingdom in human souls; fight as a king's child would; and remember that the days of your exile will pass quickly, and with them the possibility of earning merit for heaven. I expect from you, My child, a**

great number of souls who will glorify My mercy for all eternity (1489).

S. Faustina: (P.) Every soul You have entrusted to me, Jesus, I will try to aid with prayer and sacrifice, so that Your grace can work in them. O great lover of souls, my Jesus, I thank You for this immense confidence with which You have deigned to place souls in our care (245).

All: Grant, Merciful Lord, that not even one of those souls which You have entrusted to me be lost.

C. You, who suffered wounds for us,

P. Christ Jesus, have mercy on us.

Sung Verse: *Christ, when Thou shalt call me hence,*
Be Thy Mother my defense,
Be Thy Cross my victory.

Closing Prayer

All: My Jesus, my only hope, I thank You for this book which You opened to the eyes of my soul. This book is Your Passion, undertaken out of love for me. From this book, I learn how to love God and souls. This book contains inexhaustible treasures. O Jesus, how few souls understand You in Your martyrdom of love. Happy the soul that has come to understand the love of the heart of Jesus!

For the intentions of the Holy Father
Our Father … . Hail Mary … . Glory Be ….

Prayer in Honor of the Holy Cross

God our Father, in obedience to You
Your only Son accepted death on the cross
for the salvation of mankind.
We acknowledge the mystery of the cross on earth.
May we receive the gift of redemption in heaven.
We ask this through our Lord Jesus Christ, Your Son,
Who lives and reigns with You and the Holy Spirit
one God, for ever and ever. Amen

Veneration of the relic of the Holy Cross

Notes

Notes

Notes

Notes

Notes

Another Booklet and a Video from the Shrine

The National Shrine of The Divine Mercy
Three O'clock Hour Prayerbook
Arranged and Introduced by the Rector of the National Shrine of The Divine Mercy

Thousands of pilgrims visit the National Shrine every year to receive the Sacraments and to participate in the Three O'clock Hour devotions to Jesus, The Divine Mercy. Now, through this booklet, you can join the Marians at the National Shrine in praying to The Divine Mercy at the Three O'clock Hour every day!

The booklet provides an explanation of 3 p.m. as the "Hour of Great Mercy." It also explains the Divine Mercy Novena and Chaplet, which are both prayed at 3 p.m. The complete text of the prayers recited at the National Shrine during this hour are included: St. Faustina's Prayer for Sinners, the Divine Mercy Novena, the Chaplet, A Prayer for Divine Mercy, a Benediction Hymn and the Divine Mercy Praises, and the Chaplet in Spanish, French, Polish, and Italian. An ideal resource for your parish or your home.

Booklet, 32 pages.   **17082**

The Chaplet of Divine Mercy in Song
Live from: the National Shrine of The Divine Mercy
Produced by Trish Short in Collaboration with the Marians and Eucharistic Apostles of The Divine Mercy

Here is a contemporary, fresh version of the Chaplet of Divine Mercy — a prayer that pleads God's mercy on the whole world. This sung version opens with a slow, graceful piano that leads to a crescendo with guitar and percussion. As the melody builds and the background vocals blend in, the Chaplet turns into a soaring, heartfelt prayer imploring heaven for God's redeeming love. This Chaplet was filmed live at the National Shrine with the goal of sharing this urgent message of mercy with people of every background, faith, and culture.

VHS Video, 26 minutes   **VCDM**